No Rhythm Blues

and other poems

Seth A. Tribble

*To everyone who's loved
me in spite of myself*

Table of Contents

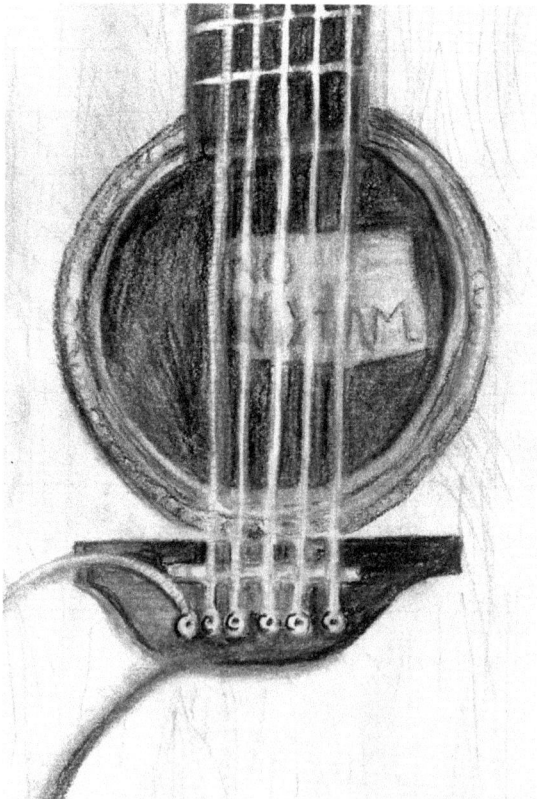

The Generation of My Generation

I know we're not Lost

We know right where we are

And we're not a bunch of Beatniks

We don't wanna burn bright & out

We're not the fucking hippies

We know we can't change shit

But

We're not nothing anymore

And our incoherent mewlings

Aren't for lack of articulation

We're a square peg

With no hole of any shape

We used to scream "wake up!

It's our turn! Can we have a try?"

But you stuffed rittlin in our mouths

We are the silent solemn cynics

A disparate band of mutes

Who didn't get boo'd

When we got off the plane

We didn't get anyone.

Not a Hanky-waving housewife

Or even angry protestor in sight

Did you forget there was a war on?

Or did you leave your opinion

In your other pants?

It's like we're kids again

And even bad attention

Is better than none

There's no generation like this one

With no generation to speak of

We're the hungry generation

Attention-starved mallrats

Grown to soul-starved latchkeys

Love-sick and forlorn

Wisdom-deprived and fat on knowledge

We consume on sight

Hedonists without filling

Or pleasure really

It's all a part of the grind

That's just how we think life is.

We learned it from watching you

Eat and drink and smoke

And sing and learn and play

Our fill but really, who gives a fuck?

Why fight the establishment

When we know it will eat us too

Like it did our hippie-turned-broker dad

We got no voice, no beatking

No prophet, no sutra

And all our drugs are boring

Hemmingway's dead

Kerouac's dead

Ginsburg, Bukowski and Thompson

So who's gonna be the voice

Of my revolution?

It's sure as shit not Kanye

And my throat is sore from shouting

Busywork

Race to times

That can't be caught

Events that blend

Blurring the boundaries

Of importance

Paying out my effort

For something I can't see

Not an honest labor

Earning honest wage

Just an inconsequential series

Soon forgotten

Working to a greater good

I guess

It just seems so little

When AIDS is still around

And soldiers die again and again

But I've got things to do today

Best to put it out of mind

Out of sight, after all.

The Wanting

Waves drain and crash

Find and crash again

Wash and fade

To rush upon the will again

And take a bit away

To leave in peace

A weakling wall

With Wanting waiting

At its core and without

Crashing again

Patient in its violence

Pounding out its constant beat

Knowing that this stone

Disciplined humility

Will turn to vanity

Someday

Soon, it will take you out to sea…

50mg Siddhartha

Terrible weeds

Thorns and brambles

Tearing the light

From the sky

Shadows and fog

Tremble and terror

Muted pastels

In the hall

Feeling the nothing

Rending the texture

Off my hunger

For all the desire

Milligram Buddha

Three times a day

As needed for nirvana

With food and regular therapy

No Rhythm Blues

"Dear God, make me a writer again!" –Jack Kerouac

Gone!

It's gone!

I got nothin' left

But the passion and blue

My lady sure is pretty

And she loves me true

I love her too

With my little black book

Pen in hand and nothin' in my head

No booze in my belly or junk in my blood

It's boiling roiling toiling still trying

To find in me

Capacity

But opacity still prevents

Simplest expression

Serving soulless sentences

Still stinging singing slave songs

Old and not of my making

Marking maps in my mind

Meandering mesmerized

Looking lost like little latchkey I am

Always assuming assurance

Is right round the bend

But blended blunders blind my third eye

And still the only thing to write

Is true

I'm blue

And resorting to rhyme

Makes me angry

It's not me!

Never will be!

But there it is, me

Contradicting me

And my ability to self-deny

But I try and that's what's important

The never being satisfied

Always being hungry for new

And interesting ways to fuck it all up

But the only way

Tried and true is to

Stop

But I'm stuck

Striving standing driving on

To make something real enough

To put down on paper

I got too much technology, too little time

And an opinion for every asshole who asks

I'm over-occupied and still

Somehow underachieving

Perceiving myself in a way I haven't

For quite some time now

As something worth more

Than an epitaph or obituary

Tragically understated

Survived by half-filled notebooks

And scraps of napkin

Scratched upon in late-night hours

In a corner of obscurity

And security made of my own

Self doubt stained with halos

Of long dried coffee and ink

Smudged with fingerprints

And now complacency gives way

To invasions of ambition

And an all-consuming desire

Don't desire, be desired

Desire drives disappointment

And at times it was better to be the body wanted

Than cold outside

And I was good at that too

So before the onslaught of wanting

Beset by the urge to retreat

I shake

And she shakes with me

Like leaves in a storm me and my muse

Until I see my enemy

And take her hand

This is where I make my stand

In this old apartment

This dirty diner

This one more page

Swelling to anthems

Pages of victory

And another fruitful night

Of trite and stunted little words

Trying desperately to be

The fulfillment of all those things I want

But can't stomach to try

And by the time I've come to the point

When I should stop wanting

More!

Like a face of avarice

And I am amiss

Something's coming

I can hear its footprints

Down the hall

The resolutions sought

Were all the scary monsters

In my childhood closet

Come to take my soul

And my notebooks and my pens!

And all my empty pages!

And leave me with the wanting!

That damnable desire

To express that me I want to be

In words cryptic hodgepodge

So the only ones understanding

Are the ones I want to understand

And hand in hand we face the fact

That we are beautiful!

And so is this twisted, wretched world

But I can't.

Not right now.

I'm blue.

My Last Prayer

God!

You got it all wrong!

You made a man for his beauty

And you gave him rage

He's made his make from rage

He's called down cars

And bombs and hate

He walks the girders and stories

Of buildings five thousand feet high

And knocks them down with lives

You twisted his tongues

So he twisted your words

He kills with them

Makes bullets with them

Fires the black man with them

And fucks the homosexual ass with them

There's a hole in them

Shaped like the thing you made

And we filled it with rage

And page after page is filled

With the bile and beer-foam of it

We made a new You to fit in our image

And we killed the thought we were made to think

That thing that sublime

That perfect shape

Where soul is no less body than thought

And a cat's eye from the dark closet

We remind him of the box

Where his existence makes mockery of our sight

And sound the eternal perennial flavor

Of feeling that small sweet ball

We all keep in our pocket

Made of spikes and fluff and hurt and love

That chaos

That terminal feeling

That fearful reckoning of realization

We exist

What do you say, God?

Where are your prophets and oracles?

Where are your fanfare playing trumpeters

And angels?

Where is your wisdom?

Where is your son

Whose followers cast stones

When they're lonely?

What time do you have?

Where is your pocket watch running down to the end?

Or the interminable silence of why?

What will I teach my son of you

When my brother is a pile of shit?

What heroes do we have?

Why did they die?

Would we worship their killers?

Or make out to be demons

Ones whose families get eaten by their false god?

A brown man killed me

I killed him back

We did this a thousand times

Until my child suffers for the struggle

And now a life?

A tiny thing of light in the womb?

And I this dark pathetic sobbing mass

This rejecter of rage

Enabler of conmen and bitches

The high road man

Trampled by my ideals and desires

For peace and happy gentle lovingness

This murderer of fanatics and kindred souls

This blatant Coward in the face of the world

And its rage

Fuck!

Haphazard terror screaming memories

And trees outside windows long neglected

Forgotten courage

Forgotten passion

Forgotten poetry

Feeling forwardly pissed off progressions of hate

And me! I cannot fathom!

I fear and tear apart my inner-most failings

And me along with them

And I to be a teacher?

A guide for this thing of absolute purity?

Wear your helmet!

Drink your water!

The world will eat you!

And I must prevent it!

A tempest!

A fire!

And flailing of steel and words!

Battering rams torn from their mountings

Rage!

I will not show it this grim portrait

As the light slowly fades from my mind

I must excel

I must defeat

I must nurture and teach and protect.

I'm going to be a daddy.

Down Southbound

I dream of trains

The clacking travel rhythm

World beneath, rolling by

With time to think

No place to fall

The well-to-do sleeper cars

Rocking comfortable like babies

Silver blue California fields

Out the window

Cold coming through glass

A sudden frightful roar

Of freight train heading north

Out of Sacramento

A road trip midnight town

An old speakeasy hotel town

Waking up in a bridal suite

With wrecked memories of

A maybe night before

Diner car coffee

In plastic cups and familiar carbon

Tang in the bottom of the mug

Moving memories

Railroad recollections

Driving ancient iron in my bones

Twisting mountain Chinese steel

Cuddled stranger close

Against the passing snow

Five-hundred mile romance

Thin, upward smile

Sultry Parisian laugh

And a phone number with

A few too many digits

A backpack far too big

For slender dreadlock-draped waist

She got off in San Francisco

I continued on

Down the rails

Along the pulse

Feeling the world breathe

As the light peeks out

Over LA mountain dawn

And I miss the cold home

In the brown salt chill

Gremlins

I had a something inside me

I tried to catch it

But it bit my wounded knee

It ran out of me

It bit her too

I tried to catch it

We ran in the circles

Plato told me about

The ones I drew in grade school

I had the something cornered

Till it jumped in my head

I knew it was a she

But it was me

I hurt it and I hate it

This thing that was me

Is me

I knew it was tired

I was too

But she flew away

I did this

The horrible thing

What was this thing

The me I knew I was?

This villain I knew I could be

It frolicked in my nightmares

It drew my fears in pencil

On a cheap chalkboard

I threw it out

It punished me for that

It was patient

And I died

Why I Occupy No More

In a dripping haze

Of martyred days

We filled the streets with joy and rage

We found a voice, and found a stage

And told the world we'd turned a page

But at home the ties

Our family's blind

And fuck you for saying otherwise

This time the tines

Of clever lines

Are filling up my hopeful mind

And turning it into a factory

A broken causes phylactery

And a glutton for gloried defeat

To tear gas and panicked retreat

Though the songs we will always repeat

The cause lays like glass in the street

So home we go

And wind up alone

For things we said

And should have known

Were a lie

And the we that we were's now an I

'Coz I tried too hard to try

And the me that I was has died

And I killed him

Again and again

With each cause and each stand

To block out the sand

And now that I am

All alone and a man

I know where I always go wrong

It isn't in romance or song

It's in feeling belief

That I can achieve

Any more than anyone else

'Coz I think way too highly of self

Just like every young punk in that park

Huddled in close in the dark

And saying we're quitters

But we're not baby-sitters

To some kid with a Black Flag tattoo

Who knows shit 'coz he's 22

He's screaming and crying

Like he's fucking dying

Or like it's the first time he's been maced

And our moral high ground is erased

When he throws shit at cops

And goes home when they stop

Filming him holding his sign

And it's him that'll get the air time

So fuck it, I'm done

I've marched and I've sung

I know what I've lost

And what can be won

I've a child to feed

And work to be done

Not out of greed

But 'coz I love my son

And no one will benefit from this.

Thursday Morning Blues

Like a crowbar to the head

The wine wakes me

Asking in no uncertain terms

"Why the good green fuck

Did you do that last night?"

An empty bottle

My bedmate shocks

Cold against my cock

When I try to stretch away

Awakeness

The first thing to touch me there

Other than pants or my hand

In far too long

Recoil and yelp

Images of Iraqi snakes

Slither clear through hazy

Half-memories of brown-bagging

In my own living room

With cloud-shrouded moon

Bursting in through

The broken blinds

A freeze-frame firework

Washed up on linoleum shoals

Fall out of bed

Try to find my head

And some pants that don't stink

Maybe something to eat

Then the disaster

Falls into focus

I upended my table

At some point

A quiet monument

To the kind of night

I might have had

Had I been a bit more sad

And I smile

My neatly stacked files

Confetti-cannon cover the floor

Someone made it rain, bitches

There isn't any more carnage

Just an isolated incident

Those motherfuckers

Won't get a goddamn thing from me

Apparently

Pull on last night's sweater

Pull open the curtain

A grey-blue sea spills in

Clouds shored by grey-green

City-scape crashing foaming

Park trees frozen reaching

Fingers through misty way-too-early

Morning

Thank Christ I got drunk last night

Or I might not appreciate it

I slip through my still-drunk door

Take five steps

What'd I forget?

My keys of course

Spin and rush

Keep spinning

But beat the latch

And hatch a craving

Not for smoke

Did I smoke?

My breath tastes clean

But eggs sure sound nice

I have some in my ice-box

But they aren't out there

In the sea-breeze morning

And I'm too fucking lazy anyway

Stagger past the super "hello"

And try to avoid a conversation

Though she's stationed by the sign

Telling us to pick up our dogs' shit

She must have made a new one

I can't be bothered

I don't own a dog

I zigzag wander wondering

Why the hell I hurt so bad

Until I remember the bottle I had

And emptied out

Filled my brain with wine

Which traded places with

Whatever was in there

At the time

So now I have a bottle

Full of painful memories

Cuddled still in blankets

Wrapped to startle me again

When I go back to bed

And in my head I still see

Waves

Rising through a wine-soaked haze

And crashing like a sailor's calling

To the sea or like falling

In love

But a bus' rumbling

Breaks my stumbling

Stride. I've arrived

And poured through the door

Like a liquid wanting more

Substance to my solidity

My booth is open

Are you kidding me?

Coffee's already there

Waitress is on the ball

I don't even have to call

For more. She's there

I must look like shit

Or she knows I leave a big tip

If I never see the bottom

Of the mug and the food is done quick

Which it is

I thank her profusely

Find out she's confused me

For someone else

I leave a big tip anyway

I got things I gotta do today

But the bus is ten minutes late

'Coz the fuckers who legislate

Can never agree

On the most basic things

The proposition would pass

If they pull their head...

Here it comes!

At last!

But I'm not complaining

It's not even raining

And really I'm paining

Myself

Headphones on in the

Misty post-dawn burning away

Into dusty coated saffron day

Driver reminds me to pay

Fuck, I gotta quit drinking

Something's festering stinking

Up the place

Shit, is that me?

Did I take a shower?

Goddammit no I didn't

And I can't stay hidden

'Coz I'm the only one here

Why does it smell like beer?

Did I drink beer last night?

I can't see the driver's eyes

He's wearing sunglasses

It's not even that bright

It took some time to realize

He's just as hung over as me

For some reason that doesn't feel

That much better

Now I'm in a hurry to get there

Before someone dies

Ah, I don't care, this is nice

At least I didn't have to drive

But this is my stop

Thank Christ I'm hung over

Makes all this seem almost

Interesting

Names Carved Into a Painted Banister

I found her note in the bathroom cabinet

It smelled of mildew and stale cleaners

In a browned envelope hidden by the S-bend

Addressed to "No one in particular"

She used a purple gel pen to tickle the face

With delicate swirls like fingers

On a cheek long forgotten

It trembled with me when I cracked the brittle glue

Just a single blue-lined page

Etched with that familiar hue

I got to know her like a lover

She treated the lines like sheets

She made love to me in purple ink

She told me how she lost me

How she never got me back

She lost her friends and family

So she calls to me through years

In a page folded neatly

To stave of the lonely gnaw

She hadn't spoken to anyone

And paid her rent through the slot

I had to avert my eyes

From the naked last line

She told me she loved me

She had left me pieces

Hidden here for me to find

And hoped the whole would be found

Before she started to stink

I spoke aloud to her signature

"Suzanne, I wish you weren't so sad"

I found her name carved

Into our 4th floor banister

I scratched out the paint

And signed beside her

She may not know it

But she'll never be alone

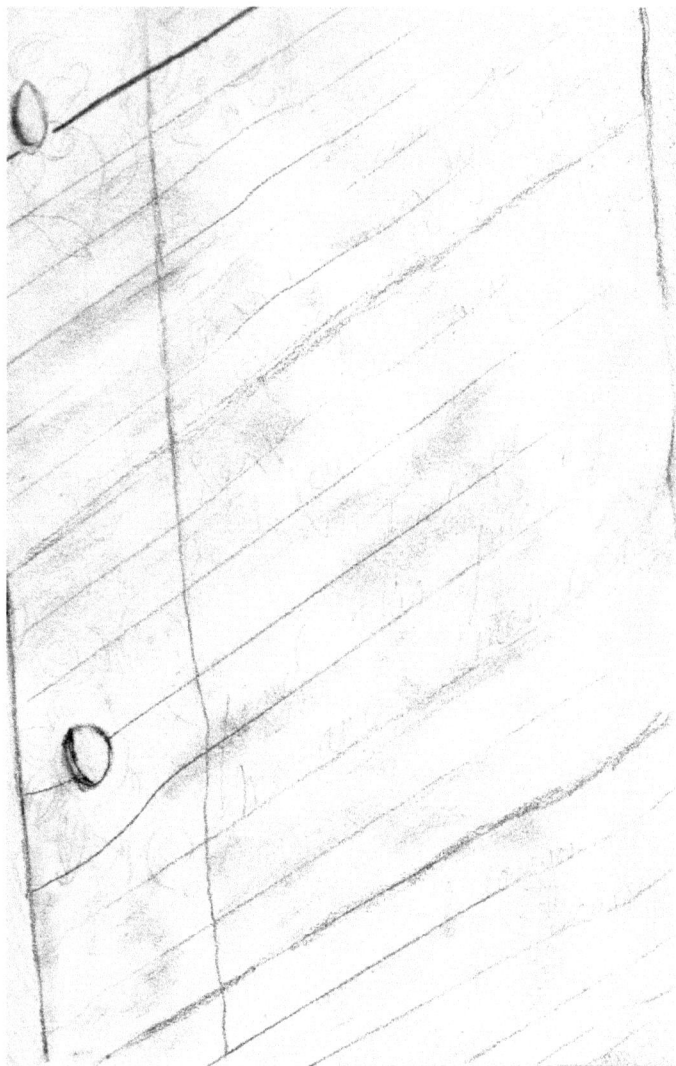

Loud Music and an Open Road

Cracked pavement driving drums

Finding focus in rolling landscape melodies

Voices blended like tree trunks and telephone poles

Passing at 70 miles an hour

A hopeful harmony

Loud music and an open road

Noise and voice and sight collide

Leaving behind the quiet grey

For soaring peaks seen from passes

And girls with hair like cinnamon singing

Into ears ripe for hearing that happy wind

And an engine tugging to run

With a baritone register organ pipe

Supporting a banjo picking just beyond earshot

Rushing into the forefront

A staccato signpost signaling ascent

Into climax as we climb this hill

A choir of pines cloaked in robes of gentle snow

Waits to strike a chord at the crest

Sending chills down spines

Warmed by sunbeams filtered

By traffic-jam clouds

Capping timpani mountaintops

Concession Stands at Murder Scenes

I can't sleep for the life of me

I feel like a deadweight hammer falls

Whenever my eyes are heavy

When I'm drunk sometimes I can manage

To slip between the dreams

Wake up refreshed and feel, but

Most nights, I'm too scared of me

I need to be watched

Like an animal

Or a baby on a ledge

It's a woodcarving world between weekends

Hard, unmoving shapes go only so deep

The horizon crowds up through half of things

An opaque barrier to block my mind

From reaching all possibilities

With sleep, I could see behind them

But when I dream, my eyes go dark

Like the silence before a snuff film

A pensive, ghastly wait for something awful

I can never sit through them

My mind ejects me from the theater

While I'm grateful for the relief

I'm tied to the seat

And the management will want it back

When I close my eyes again.

Five Haikus on Traveling

The road flower wilts
When running feet go silent
Wind is their sunshine

Roman silent roads
Their dust does not lay quiet
Stories echo still

Train car love story
Though the lover is not flesh
She is the journey

Happy thin sole shoes
With many miles beneath them
And many more yet

Roots of stones are still
They have no life to move them
Our roots are running

St. Joseph Is Unemployed

Saint Joseph hangs flowers

On his neighbors' doors

With black flag ribbons

A May Day bouquet to mourn

The jobs they don't have

Anymore

The Missing Haymarket

Bullet holes in telephone Maypoles

A memory of 1886

But while the world marches

We dance

Talks on loyalty

And an American tradition

They'd rather us remember

Seattle is Rioting Again

Protective mothers, jilted lovers

And other things equally dangerous

Don't compare for those who dare

Who try to take the street from us

My Heart Beats Slow

When I want someone

No one knows

I hold silent my desire

Jealously guard this loneliness

Keep it for another tomorrow

To find a way I can be enough

I keep a carving of myself

Laying on my empty bed

Curled around a space someone might go

If any person could fit there

In the purpose-built hole

Between a bottle and a bad memory

A shaking head with a bolted-on grimace

To rest on invisible shoulder

And a wounded knee to cradle

Feet that never crossed my doorway

Carved in my bones

Just beneath my chest

An intricate linework in my sternum

Flipped around for my heart to admire

And beat more slowly

Pressed against tar-scarred lungs

Resting on battered-liver bed

In anticipation of one more memory

To come down the pipe like a wood maul

And crack it open again

So I tremble alone

And my heart beats slow

The War Cry of the Meek

They'll always hate us for who we are

Leave us weeping, battered, scarred

'Coz we're fags, fat-asses & retards

And they think we deserve it anyway

It's ok

To hate a man for being gay

Or who listens to him when he prays

And make him feel alone

Like he's really on his own

But he's not.

They may not desist

When we resist

But we'll raise our beaten, bloody fists

Not to fight, but to insist

That we are not alone in this

So make a friend, make a plan

In kindness we must take our stand

To fight the fire, we must truly admire

Each other and never give in

We don't have to fight to win

Just keep being

We'll grind them down 'till the world turns around

And we can be the lingering sound

'Coz we faced the hate of untempered rage

And we always stood our ground

They might break our bones and black our eyes

But we will never compromise

We must dissent

Take pride in what makes us different

Simply because we must

And they can never take ourselves from us

An Aging Question

Pot-bellied pint

Or thereabouts

Searching for another

Glass to knock up against

In joyful celebration

That another pint exists

In another hand

Crafted just as exquisite

By the cosmos that made mine

And when our fingers collide

Our faces will be filled

With beer and teeth

That stand a good chance

Of staying put all night

'Coz I'm too old

Anymore in any case

To want to knock any out

And the bars I inhabit these days

Are markedly quieter

Than the ones that used to get my money

I'm slowing down

And I haven't decided

Whether or not that's a good thing.

The Offering

A coal fire purge

Smelting away damage

Of a crackle kindling past

Wild flame hair flayed

Open like arms accepting

Consuming serenity

Buddha beads untouched

By licking conflagration

Transitioning perspective

The sacrifice becomes

The flame

And wood and earth burn away

A miserly meandering

Afterthought life

Bursts into radiant intention

A violent emigration

Into invariable aspiration

And ambition

To be both burned

And the burning

Blinders

I fell into an excess

Of arrogant almosts

Altruistic ambitions

With awful aftershocks

And I'm my own antagonist

Trying anything to avoid

Ignoble aspiration

But ignorant of anything

Metaphorically ambulatory

Too mindful of miniscule

Metrics made more important

By my resilient rhetoric

Resoundingly resolute

Restricting response to

Redirect discussion

Dissolving into diatribes

Of my own design

Detracting from dilemmas

Which are actually important

And might improve me

Another Nervous Morning

I've been crying in my sleep again

I can see the salt drops on my face

In an early morning mirror

And the dog is disconcerted

There's a nervous energy in the air

And my shakes form my hands

Into shapes suited to hold a glass

So I scurry through breakfast

To go get some smokes

And get enough of those down

Before I go be a daddy

And try my best not to fuck up

My kid with this simmering

Startle response to something

I don't remember dreaming

But will linger with me

Until something takes its place

In the back of my brain

When I can take stock

Of this torturous trembling

Or willingly wondering

If I'll ever be alright

At least I don't remember

The dreams anymore

That's something to consider

When I wonder whether

Improvement is within

My capacity

Given a long enough timeframe

Special Thanks to Jefri Peters, Michelle Lepori, Evan Senn and Madelene Susan.

Sketches by Michelle Lepori.

"The Offering" (mixed media on canvas) by Madelene Susan.

Photography by Jefri Peters.

www.ingramcontent.com/pod-product-compliance
Lightning Source LLC
Chambersburg PA
CBHW060707030426
42337CB00017B/2793